To Alex
and his crazy genius

ELEPHANTS CAN PAINT TOO!

PICTURES AND TEXT BY KATYA ARNOLD

Atheneum Books for Young Readers   New York • London • Toronto • Sydney

I teach in two schools.
One is in the city.

The other is in the jungle.

Some
of my students
have
hands.

Others have
trunks.

The elephant's trunk is both a hand and a nose. Not only can a trunk pick things up, it can smell, snore, trumpet, purr, drink, and spray. Elephants also use their trunks to communicate in a kind of sign language. A young elephant sucks its trunk the way babies suck their thumbs.

Elephants are vegetarians that eat grass, leaves, twigs, and fruit. They also like human food, especially ice cream. Each day they eat about three hundred pounds of food (as much as twelve cows eat) and drink thirty-five gallons of water (as much as a whole bathtub full). They use their trunks to put the food into their mouths and to slurp up the water.

Some students eat
grass.

Others eat
peanut butter
and jelly.

But they *all* love
cookies.

And
they all
like to
be
with
their
friends.

Young elephants play a lot. They wrestle, climb on each other, and just act plain silly. They talk to each other, with sounds people cannot hear. They can also scream and even cry tears when they are sad.

Time
for
art
class.

Elephants in Asia have worked with people for four thousand years. They've hauled huge stones and logs and were used in wars as a kind of tank that frightened enemies because of their size. Now they can be seen in parades and in circuses and carrying people in special parks. Only recently have they become artists. Like children, elephants learn from their elders and brothers and sisters. They can also learn from us.

First I give each student a brush.

Elephants live as long as people do. By age three, most Asian elephants have already learned a lot of commands, such as "Come," "Bring it," "Stop," and "Lie down." Some elephants learn to hold a brush right away. Others take a week or two.

Look
at how many
ways
there are
to hold it.

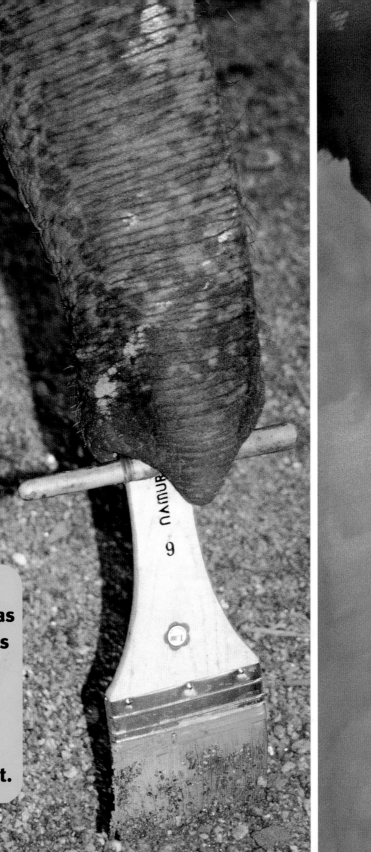

Elephants have 150,000 muscles
in their trunks. (Our entire body has
only 639 muscles.) Some elephants
hold the brush by wrapping their
trunks around it. Others hold it
inside their trunks. If an elephant
throws the brush away or eats it,
he probably won't become an artist.

Now let's paint!

After the teacher guides the elephant's trunk to the paper and says, "Touch!" some elephants drag the brush over the paper. Others dab. If the teacher points and says, "Make a line up here," they do. When they want a new color, they give the brush to the teacher. Some paint for a few minutes. Others paint for as long as an hour. If they are tired or bored, they drop the brush and walk away.

These students like to paint dots.

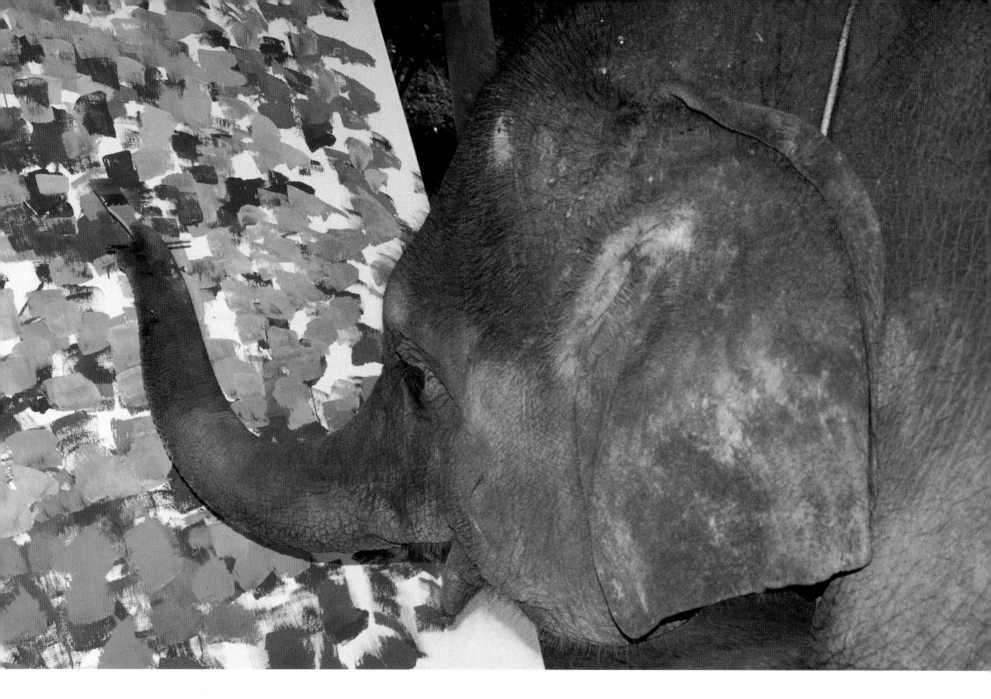

Each elephant's painting is different. Some paint with wiggly lines. Some with spots. Some paint only in the middle of the paper. Others put paint everywhere. They like to paint. Sometimes even when class is finished and the teacher is cleaning up, they grab for the brush to keep painting.

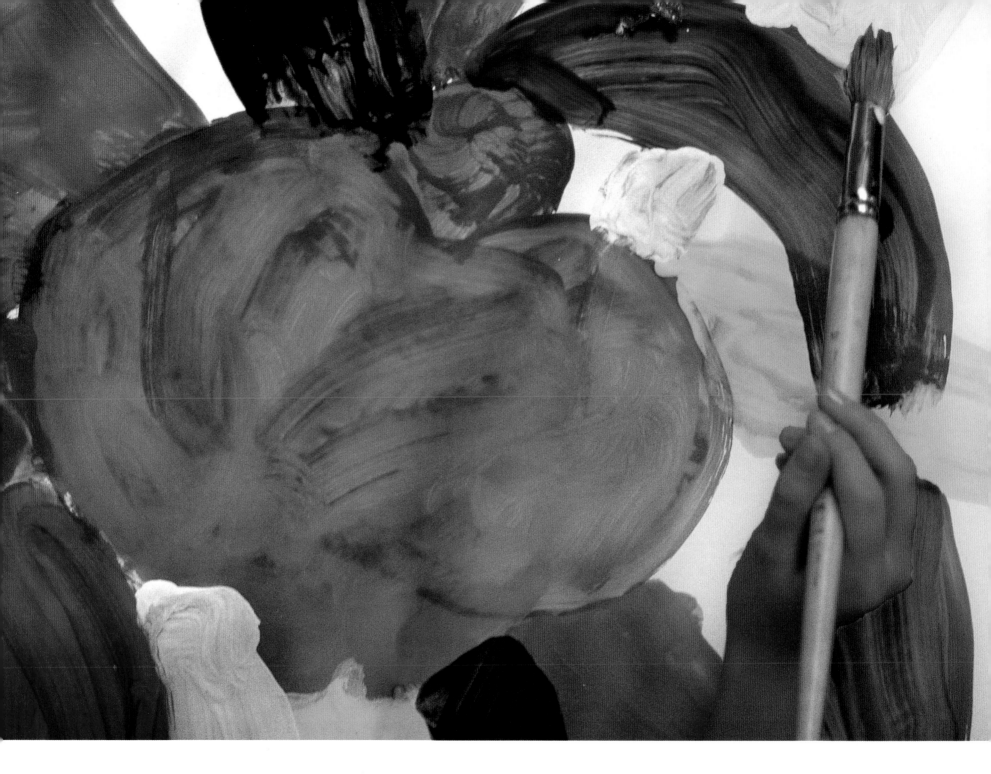

These students like

bright colors.

Wow!
These students can paint
flowers.

Most elephants don't paint real things. They paint colored strokes. But some elephants paint trees and flowers. It takes them about three years to learn. Whatever they paint, it helps to praise them and reward them with a treat. (Children learn to paint much faster than elephants do.)

Everyone has

their own style.

Anything can happen when the teacher isn't looking.

Young elephants can misbehave. They grab each other's tails, steal fruit from your pocket, snatch the hat off your head, and run away from their mothers, who then spank them with their trunks. Sometimes they spray their teacher with water.

Time
to
clean
up.
Remember
to wash
between
your
toes.

Elephants bathe every day. Like children, they love water. Although an elephant can weigh as much as six cars, all are good swimmers. Using their trunk as a snorkel, they can swim up to thirty miles without resting.

Art class
is over.
All my
students
can
paint
and
be proud!

Exhibitions of elephant art in Japan, Italy, England, and the United States show people all over the world how amazing the elephant paintings are. A lot of people have bought elephant paintings. The money that is made is used to provide a secure and healthy life for the Asian elephants.

Author's Note

Since ancient times Asian elephants have been trained to help people. Their most important job has been to drag heavy logs from the jungle to the rivers or roads, then lift them with their tusks onto boats or trucks.

Today forests, jungles, and other wild places are being destroyed and developed for human use. Less forest means there is less space for wild animals. It also causes a change in the region's climate. Some countries, like Thailand, realized this and stopped cutting trees. But it has caused a new problem: what to do with Thailand's three thousand domesticated elephants who have lost their jobs hauling felled trees? Without work, the elephants cannot earn their keep. As a result they are dying out.

An artist in New York, Alex Melamid, decided to help the elephants. Because I am an art teacher as well as an artist, I went along with Alex (my husband) to Thailand, India, and Cambodia, to teach the elephants what we know best— painting. Together we established painting schools where we trained approximately thirty elephants and supplied their keepers with art materials and ideas about how to keep the project going. Teaching elephants and spending time close to them has been one of the most beautiful and thrilling experiences of our lives.

In order to sell the elephant pictures, the Asian Elephant Art and Conservation Project was organized. AEACP is a nonprofit organization dedicated to saving the diminishing number of Asian elephants. It promotes and sells the work of elephant artists via its Web site, www.elephantart.com, as well as in galleries, museums, and auction houses around the world. In this way, AEACP raises funds for and increases public awareness of the plight of Asian elephants.

Part of the profits of this book will also go to help elephants. We encourage you to support the elephants by buying a painting for your home or your child's classroom or school.

Atheneum Books for Young Readers
An imprint of Simon & Schuster Children's
Publishing Division
1230 Avenue of the Americas
New York, New York 10020
Copyright © 2005 by Katya Arnold
All rights reserved, including the right of reproduction
in whole or in part in any form.
Book design by Ann Bobco
The text for this book is set in Meta.
Manufactured in China
10 9 8 7

Library of Congress Cataloging-in-Publication Data
Arnold, Katya.
Elephants can paint too! / pictures and text by
Katya Arnold.
p. cm.
ISBN 0-689-86985-1
1. Asiatic elephant—Behavior—Juvenile literature.
2. Animals as artists—Juvenile literature. I. Title.
QL737.P98A765 2005
599.67—dc22
2004017387

PHOTO CREDITS
Photography by Katya Arnold except:
Painted foot by Mia Fineman
Trunk wrapped around the brush by Jason Schmidt
Katya washing elephant's trunk and giving brush to the elephant by Alex Melamid
Endpaper and abstract painting across from kids' abstract painting by Oote Boe

ACKNOWLEDGMENTS
I must first of all thank the elephants and their mahouts for their hard work, patience, and good humor; and Alex
Melamid, without whom this project would not exist.
    I am also grateful to my students and colleagues at Saint Ann's School for their participation and support,
and to the following people who helped me so much in making this book: Max Ross, Sam Swope, Ian Frazier,
Anne Schwartz, Ann Bobco, David Ferris, Mia Fineman, Zinovy Zinik, and Yvette Lenhart.
    It would be impossible to mention everyone who worked so hard to support elephant artists, but these
generous people deserve special mention: Don RedFox, Christine Sperber, Jim Ottaway, Stuart Pivar, Rosemary
Ewing, Jennifer Essen, Linzy Emery, Greta Gruber, and Jane Bausman (1968–2001).

IN THAILAND
Her Royal Highness the Princess Galiyani, Lesley Junlankan, William Warren, Ping Amranand, and Robert Steele

CHIANG MAI
Maesa Elephant Camp; Khun Anchalee Kulmapijit, operation director; Khun Chaowalit Sae Jern and Khun
Tossapol Petcharattanakool, elephant art teachers; Rak Rae, Gongkam's mahout; Khun Chay, Kamsan's mahout;
and Khun Chien, Wanpen's mahout

KOH CHANG
Pittaya Homkrailas, operation director; and Khun Peud, Jintara's mahout

LAMPANG
Forest Industry Organization of Thailand and Richard Lair at Thai Elephant Conservation Center

SURIN
Valley of the Mool River Basin, Ta Klang Village, Abbot Haan, and Jo, Plai Chompon's personal mahout

AYUTTAYA
Ayuttaya Elephant Palace and Royal Kraal; Sompast Meepan, director; and Wittaya, Nom Chok's mahout

IN INDONESIA
BALI
Bakas Elephant Camp; Bakas Levi, owner; Abas, head mahout; and Eko, Elsa's personal mahout

BOROBUDUR JAVA
Sean Flakelar, director of the Hotel Amanjiwo; Tommy Masata, director of Kandang Gajah Camp; Sukardi, head
mahout; Intun, Sela's mahout; and Paweng, elephant keeper

IN CAMBODIA
Tamao Wildlife Rescue Center; Phnom Penh, Cambodia; Nick Marx, director; and Try Sitheng, Lucky's mahout

IN INDIA
Shafi Quraishy

IN JAPAN
Sumi Hayashi, Kawamura Memorial Museum of Art